THE
NBA
A HISTORY OF HOOPS

Published by Creative Education
P.O. Box 227, Mankato, Minnesota 56002
Creative Education is an imprint of The Creative Company
www.thecreativecompany.us

Design and production by Christine Vanderbeek
Art direction by Rita Marshall

Printed by Corporate Graphics in the United States of America

Photographs by Dreamstime (Munktcu), Getty Images (Andrew D. Bernstein/
NBAE, Vernon Biever/NBAE, David Cannon, Hank Delespinasse/Sports
Illustrated, James Drake/Sports Illustrated, Stephen Dunn, Barry Gossage/
NBAE, Otto Greule Jr., Andy Hayt/NBAE, Jed Jacobsohn, John W. McDonough/
Sports Illustrated, Fernando Medina/NBAE, Manny Millan/Sports Illustrated,
Ronald C. Modra, NBA Photos/NBAE, Dick Raphael/Sports Illustrated,
SM/AIUEO), iStockphoto (Brandon Laufenberg)

Library of Congress Cataloging-in-Publication Data
Silverman, Steve.
The story of the Phoenix Suns / by Steve Silverman.
p. cm. — (The NBA: a history of hoops)
Includes index.
Summary: The history of the Phoenix Suns professional basketball
team from its start in 1968 to today, spotlighting the franchise's
greatest players and reliving its most dramatic moments.
ISBN 978-1-58341-958-8
1. Phoenix Suns (Basketball team)—History—Juvenile literature.
2. Basketball—Arizona—Phoenix—History—Juvenile literature. I. Title. II. Series.
GV885.52.P47S55 2010   796.323'64'0979173—dc22   2009036112

CPSIA: 120109 PO1093

First Edition
2 4 6 8 9 7 5 3 1

Page 3: Forward Jared Dudley
Pages 4–5: Center Shaquille O'Neal (jumping)

THE STORY OF THE

PHOENIX
SUNS

STEVE SILVERMAN

CREATIVE EDUCATION

CHAPTER ONE

THE SUNS RISE

Phoenix, Arizona, is the hottest of America's major cities. As late as the mid-1900s, the city was viewed almost as an oasis in the desert, as very little of the surrounding area had been built up. But it was inevitable that a community that sees the sun shine nearly 300 days a year would grow dramatically, and Phoenix did. The "Valley of the Sun" became an appealing destination for many, including people from northern states who wanted to get out of the cold and into the southwestern United States' dry warmth.

Arizona's capital city grew most dramatically in the 1950s and '60s. It was then, just after the Phoenix metropolitan area's population exceeded one million, that a group of investors—including singer Andy Williams, actor Tony Curtis, and composer Henry Mancini—helped convince the National Basketball Association (NBA) to grant the city an expansion franchise that would take the court for the first time in 1968. The club's owners then held a "name the team" contest that drew 28,000 entries from Arizona fans. The winning entry was, fittingly, the Suns, and the team began play as Phoenix's first major sports franchise.

The city of Phoenix experienced a population boom in the mid-1900s, thanks in part to improvements in air conditioning technology.

The Suns' first season was typical of that of most expansion teams. Head coach Johnny "Red" Kerr had an unremarkable roster of play- ers with which to work, as the Suns featured mainly players who had been cast off from other NBA franchises. The best of the lot were guards Dick Van Arsdale and Gail Goodrich. Van Arsdale had been a backup with the New York Knicks, while Goodrich had played for the Los Angeles Lakers. Both proved to be solid scorers, averaging more than 20 points per game in 1968–69.

The first-year Suns were a decent offensive team, averaging 111.7 points per game, which ranked 8th in the 14-team league. Defensively, though, Phoenix struggled, surrendering more than 120 points per game. By the end of that first season, the Suns were 16–66. Still, Arizona fans loved the club, filling the seats at Veterans Memorial Coliseum. "I didn't know how long we would last," said Coach Kerr. "I didn't know if people actually cared about basketball and would come out to the games. But they did, and they loved it."

The Suns would rise higher in the next three seasons, starting with a berth in the 1970 Western Division playoffs. This improvement was due

THE TOSS OF A COIN

The Bucks' Lew Alcindor shoots over the Suns' Neal Walk.

A 16–66 RECORD IN THE SUNS' FIRST SEASON WAS DIFFICULT FOR SOME PHOENIX FANS TO TAKE, BUT BY FINISHING WITH THE WORST RECORD IN THE WESTERN DIVISION, THE TEAM EARNED A CHANCE TO GET THE FIRST PICK IN THE 1969 NBA DRAFT. And in that draft, there was a huge prize looming: sensational University of California, Los Angeles (UCLA) center Lew Alcindor. Unfortunately, to get Alcindor (who would later change his name to Kareem Abdul-Jabbar), the Suns had to win a coin toss over the Milwaukee Bucks, a fellow expansion team who owned the Eastern Division's worst mark. The Bucks won the toss and took Alcindor (who would lead them to the 1971 NBA title), and the Suns settled for center Neal Walk. While Walk would have a respectable career, averaging 14.7 points per game in 5 seasons for Phoenix, the Suns would always wonder "What if?" "We had a group of young guys that would have fit perfectly with Alcindor," said Suns general manager Jerry Colangelo. "We would have been in a prime position to have a good long run if we had won that coin flip."

largely to the addition of forward Connie Hawkins, who came aboard in 1969. Hawkins was an electrifying player who consistently swooped to the basket to unleash an array of crowd-pleasing dunks. Hawkins's game consisted of much more than just his skywalking act, though; he was also a great passer, using his long arms and huge hands to thread pinpoint passes to teammates cutting to the hoop.

Some fans criticized Hawkins as a showoff, and others said that the time he had spent away from the NBA (having been blackballed from the league for most of the '60s after his name came up in unsubstantiated gambling rumors) had taken something from his game. Knicks coach Red Holzman, for one, dismissed such talk as ridiculous. "Hawkins is a complete player," he said. "You have to like him, because he plays both ends of the floor. I'd hate to see him get any better. He's too good now."

With Hawkins and fellow forward Paul Silas leading the way, the Suns went 48–34 in 1970–71. However, playing in the tough Midwest Division of the newly formed Western Conference, that record was not good enough for a postseason berth. The club's improvement continued the following year with a 49–33 record, but Phoenix again missed the playoffs, finishing behind the Milwaukee Bucks and Chicago Bulls.

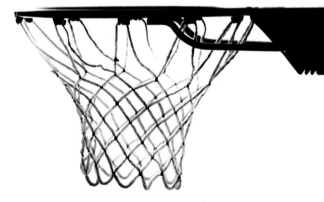

Although never known as an elite scorer, Paul Silas became a star thanks to his devotion to excellence as a rebounder and defender.

CONNIE HAWKINS

MOST BASKETBALL FANS HAD HEARD OF A LEGEND NAMED CONNIE HAWKINS BEFORE THEY EVER SAW HIM PLAY. Hawkins, a terrific high school and playground player from New York City, was at the University of Iowa finishing his freshman season in 1961 when reports surfaced that Hawkins had associated with known gamblers, hinting that he had "thrown," or intentionally lost, games. None of the allegations were proven, yet he was banned from both the university and the NBA. Finally given new life at the NBA level when the ban was lifted in 1969, the highflying Hawkins came to the Suns with guns blazing. An extraordinary leaper with jaw-dropping athleticism, Hawkins was also a hard worker who averaged 24.6 points and 10.4 rebounds a game in his first NBA season. He would go on to assemble four more memorable seasons in Phoenix before moving on to join the Lakers. "He was the first guy on that Dr. J–Michael Jordan level," NBA coach Doug Moe later said, referencing two of the game's most electrifying players. "Long strides. Hold it in one hand. Wheel it around. Nobody could match him."

CHAPTER TWO

TO THE FINALS

The Suns had reason to be optimistic heading into 1972–73. They had improved their win-loss record every year, Hawkins had established himself as an NBA All-Star, and Van Arsdale continued to steady the team with his rock-solid play in the backcourt. Unfortunately, Phoenix regressed, falling back below .500, and general manager Jerry Colangelo made a coaching change, bringing in John MacLeod.

Having solidified their coaching situation (MacLeod would remain as coach for 14 seasons), the Suns started looking to upgrade their talent level, too. They did just that in the 1975 NBA Draft, picking up center Alvan Adams and point guard Ricky Sobers in the first round. With this duo's youthful energy added to the mix, Phoenix bounced back with a 42–40 season and sneaked into the 1976 postseason.

Even though he played there only two seasons, Ricky Sobers earned the lasting love of Phoenix as part of an unforgettable 1975–76 squad.

Few fans expected the Suns to make much noise in the playoffs, as they had barely mustered a winning record. But Phoenix became the story of the 1976 NBA playoffs, beating the Seattle SuperSonics in round one, then playing the defending NBA champion Golden State Warriors to a draw through six games of a best-of-seven series. Performing with a composure that belied their experience, Adams and the Suns went on the road in Game 7 and pulled off the impossible, downing the Warriors 94–86 to earn a spot in the NBA Finals.

Facing the upstart Suns in the Finals were the veteran Boston Celtics. The matchup pitted the fast-improving Adams against the Celtics' best player, aggressive center Dave Cowens. Most fans expected Cowens, who could at times resemble a raging bull on the court, to dismantle the quiet and slender Adams. But a funny thing happened as the series unfolded. Adams showed no signs of being intimidated, battling Cowens gamely at both ends of the floor. The teams split the first four games, then traveled to Boston Garden for Game 5.

That game played out as one of the most exciting in NBA history. Thanks to fine performances by Adams, Sobers, guard Paul Westphal,

and forward Gar Heard, the Suns kept pace with the Celtics late into the fourth quarter … then into not one, but two overtimes. With the screams of the Boston crowd ringing in his ears, Heard buried an incredible turnaround jumper at the end of the second overtime to tie the game at 112–112 and force yet a third extra session. Unfortunately for Suns fans, Boston then hung on for a 128–126 victory.

Two days later, Boston won Game 6 to take the championship. The Suns, despite the loss, had won league-wide respect, especially with their Game 5 heroics. "It's a game that is always in our minds," Colangelo said years later. "It's one of the most historic games ever, and it's hard not to think about it."

COURTSIDE STORIES

Curtis Perry shoots over Celtics defenders in the 1976 Finals.

THE GREATEST GAME EVER?

THE FIFTH GAME OF THE 1976 NBA FINALS BE-
TWEEN THE SUNS AND THE CELTICS HAS BEEN
CALLED THE GREATEST GAME EVER PLAYED.
Phoenix was a huge underdog in the series, but it
had just won two home games to tie the series at two
games apiece. In Boston, the confident young Suns
pushed Game 5 into a third overtime period after mak-

ing a brilliant strategic move. With time running out in
the second overtime, Phoenix guard Paul Westphal
called timeout, even though his team had none left.
The Celtics were awarded a free throw (which they
made) on a technical foul, but Phoenix was then able to
inbound the ball at center court rather than from the far
end. With the Suns trailing 112–110 with one second

left, forward Curtis Perry inbounded the ball to forward
Gar Heard, who caught it at the foul line, spun, and
launched a high-arcing shot that hit nothing but net.
Boston would win the game in the third overtime, but
Heard's shot–and the Suns' overall effort–would go
down in NBA lore.

CHAPTER THREE

THE ELECTRIC '80s

Throughout the rest of the 1970s and into the mid-1980s, Phoenix continued to put strong lineups on the court. In 1978–79, the Suns—featuring Adams, Westphal, and guards Walter Davis and Don Buse—got off to a solid start, then traded for New Orleans Jazz forward Leonard "Truck" Robinson in midseason. Robinson, as befitted his nickname, was a rugged, bruising player who established himself as a rebounding machine. The Suns finished the season 50–32, then beat the Portland Trail Blazers and Kansas City Kings in the playoffs to advance to the Western Conference finals versus the SuperSonics. Needing just one more series victory to return to the grand stage of the NBA Finals, Phoenix came up short, losing four games to three.

A pure scorer nicknamed "Sweet D," Walter Davis spent 11 seasons in a Suns uniform, making the NBA All-Star Game roster 7 times.

After 4 more seasons in which Phoenix averaged more than 50 wins a year but suffered first- or second-round playoff losses, the Suns struggled in 1983–84. They went a mere 41–41 but—as was the case in 1976—slipped into the playoffs and found their groove. With Davis providing much of the team's backcourt scoring (Westphal was sidelined by injury), and with highflying forward Larry Nance spearheading Phoenix's low-post efforts, the Suns got by Portland and the Utah Jazz in the first two rounds of the playoffs, only to fall to the Lakers in the conference finals.

In 1985–86, the Suns missed the playoffs for the first time in nine years. As they looked at their roster,

COURTSIDE STORIES

PASSING FANCY

Paul Westphal heads upcourt.

One of the most memorable such squads was the 1979–80 Suns, a team that finished with a 55–27 record. Featuring guards Paul Westphal and Walter Davis, forward Leonard "Truck" Robinson, and center Alvan Adams, the Suns were loaded with talented scorers. What made the team special, however, was its devotion to smart passing. Adams, Davis, Westphal, and point guard Don Buse each averaged four or more assists per game, making the Suns one of the most difficult teams in the league to defend. Head coach John MacLeod described the 1979–80 Suns as one of the best passing teams he was ever associated with. "You talk about passing and looking for the open man every play," MacLeod said. "I don't know that we ever had a team that did it any better than the Suns that year. It seemed like everyone got more out of making the good pass than they did hitting a shot."

**ALVAN ADAMS WAS ONE OF THE MOST UNIMPOS-
ING STARS THE NBA HAS EVER SEEN.** The Suns
knew he had a chance to be a special player, selecting
him with the fourth overall pick in the 1975 NBA Draft
after watching his stellar career unfold at the University
of Oklahoma. But early on, opposing teams' coaches
and centers would look at the 6-foot-9 and 220-pound

big man and think they were in for a field day. Not only
was Adams on the small and thin side for an NBA
center, but he was a quiet player who didn't believe in
trading hostile glares or engaging in other theatrics.
Adams made a career of proving that impression wrong.
He played a key role as the Suns advanced to the 1976
NBA Finals, earning the adoration of Phoenix fans and

respect around the league as he fought hard against
Boston's star center, Dave Cowens, in the championship series. "That was Alvan," former Suns head coach
John MacLeod later said. "He didn't necessarily look the
part, but he went out and played hard every night."

THE SUNS WERE SPUTTERING DURING THE 1987–88 SEASON. While they featured a swift and high-jumping star in forward Larry Nance, they also featured center James Edwards and forward Armen Gilliam—lead-footed and deliberate big men who slowed down the game. Phoenix was losing night after night, so coach and player personnel director Cotton Fitzsimmons decided it was time to bring in some speed, and he pulled the trigger on a trade that brought fast rookie point guard Kevin Johnson in from Cleveland along with forward Ty Corbin and center Mark West. Fitzsimmons had admired Johnson's work from afar and—while watching the Cavaliers play the Chicago Bulls and legendary guard Michael Jordan—became convinced that "KJ" was destined for stardom. Fitzsimmons noticed a look of frustration on Jordan's face one play when Johnson blazed through the lane, leaving defenders in his wake. "That's the kind of speed we needed," Fitzsimmons said. "I wanted to have him after I saw that. I knew he could be our engine, and I wanted him in a Suns uniform." Johnson would go on to become a three-time All-Star in Phoenix.

COURTSIDE STORIES

SPEED TO BURN

Kevin Johnson burns his defender.

Colangelo and Phoenix player personnel director Cotton Fitzsimmons concluded that the Suns needed more youth. And so, in 1988, they swapped experience for speed and enthusiasm by trading Nance and forward Mike Sanders to the Cleveland Cavaliers for super-quick rookie point guard Kevin Johnson, center Mark West, and forward Ty Corbin. Nance had been an All-Star in Phoenix, but the Suns rightly saw Johnson as one of the NBA's up-and-coming stars. West, the other pivotal part of the trade, was coming into his own as a fearsome rebounder and shot blocker.

Johnson, known to fans as "KJ," was a rarity—a point guard who could not only use his quickness to get open shots and score bunches of points, but one who also rarely turned the ball over and energized his teammates with his unselfish passing. "It didn't take long to know that he was special," Colangelo later said. "We knew he was a good player when we made the move, and he turned out to be better than we anticipated."

The Suns built their lineup and game plan around KJ's speed, surrounding him with teammates such as forward Tom Chambers, swingman Dan Majerle, and guards Eddie Johnson and Jeff Hornacek, all of whom could run and shoot. In 1988–89, the Suns emerged as one of the most explosive teams in the league, finishing 55–27 and marching into the playoffs with momentum. They rolled over the Denver Nuggets in three straight games before taking apart the Warriors in a round-two rout. There was nothing but confidence in the Suns' locker room as they prepared to engage the mighty Lakers in the Western Conference finals. But Los Angeles—the NBA's premier dynasty of the '80s—was still too powerful, topping Phoenix in four close games.

A second straight loss in the Western Conference finals in 1990, this time to Portland, convinced Suns management that another big move was in order. "We knew we were so close, but at the same time, there was something more that we needed," Kevin Johnson later said. "We just needed to get a little stronger … and find that toughness we needed."

COURTSIDE STORIES

THE SUNS GORILLA

The Suns Gorilla soars for a trampoline-assisted dunk.

THE PHOENIX SUNS GORILLA IS ARGUABLY THE MOST FAMOUS MASCOT IN ALL OF NORTH AMERICAN SPORTS. The furry mascot started his act with what was supposed to be a one-time-only halftime routine in a 1980 game. The fans in Phoenix's Veterans Memorial Coliseum roared louder for the Gorilla than they did for their team, and he was invited back regularly before becoming a standard part of the franchise's pregame and halftime routine. Since 1988, the man inside the costume has been Bob Woolf, a former private investigator from Boston. Woolf worked out constantly in order to be able to complete his stunts, which include leaping off a trampoline through a flaming ring of fire for a slam dunk. "In this job," Woolf said, "you never know what is going to come next. We try to give the fans just what they want—and a little more." Over the years, the Gorilla has become something of a cultural icon, even appearing in the popular *NBA Jam* video game in the 1990s. In 2005, he became a charter member of the Mascot Hall of Fame.

CHAPTER FOUR

SIR CHARLES COMES TO TOWN

By the start of the 1990s, the "run-and-gun" Suns had gone as far as KJ alone could take them. The point guard remained a speedy dynamo, but while the Suns continued to win a lot of games, they were not a legitimate title contender. In 1992, they made headlines with a transaction intended to change that, trading Hornacek, forward Tim Perry, and center Andrew Lang to the Philadelphia 76ers for All-Star forward Charles Barkley.

Barkley was a fearless, rough-and-tumble player who combined well-balanced skills with great physical strength. Known as both "The Round Mound of Rebound'" and "Sir Charles," he had been the main man in Philadelphia for years, but the 76ers were on a downhill slide. When Barkley asked to be traded, he was pleased to find himself headed to the Valley of the Sun.

Charles Barkley was a physical oddity, standing 6-foot-6 and weighing 250 pounds yet moving and leaping as nimbly as many guards.

The chemistry between KJ, Barkley, Majerle, and new head coach Paul Westphal was tremendous, and the 1992–93 Suns went a sensational 62–20 to claim the top seed in the Western Conference playoffs. Their record was best in the league, which meant that if they could reach the NBA Finals, they would have the home-court advantage over their opponent—a team everyone believed would be superstar guard Michael Jordan's Chicago Bulls.

Dreams of the Finals nearly died in the first round, though, as the Suns lost the first two games at home to the Lakers. Coach Westphal put pressure on his team by guaranteeing they would go to Los Angeles and win two games. The Suns did just that, then beat the Lakers in the decisive Game 5 at Phoenix's America West Arena.

The next round was no easier, but Phoenix ultimately beat the San Antonio Spurs in six games to earn a spot in the conference finals against Seattle. The Suns and SuperSonics split the first six games. Then, with Game 7 in Phoenix and a trip to the Finals on the line, the Suns stepped up their efforts and notched a 123–110 win. Barkley, in particular, was outstanding. The star forward declared before the game

INTRODUCING...

COTTON FITZSIMMONS

COACH
SUNS SEASONS 1970–72,
1988–92, 1995–96

COTTON FITZSIMMONS, WHO SERVED AS THE SUNS' HEAD COACH FOR THREE DIFFERENT STINTS, WAS AN AFFABLE AND CREATIVE LEADER WHO INSPIRED HIS CHARGES TO PLAY WITH CONSISTENCY AND INTENSITY. Fitzsimmons was also the Suns' director of player personnel during his second stint as head coach and was the man responsible for trading for point guard Kevin Johnson in 1988. The deal that saw the Suns swap star forward Larry Nance and another player to Cleveland for Johnson and two other players was widely criticized in Phoenix, but it changed the culture for a team that was losing both games and fan support. The Suns won 55 games in 1988–89, and Fitzsimmons was voted the NBA's Coach of the Year. Always quick with a quip, Fitzsimmons once explained his philosophy as a coach and personnel boss by saying, "You've got to be fired up with enthusiasm, or else we'll fire you with enthusiasm." After hanging up his coaching whistle, Fitzsimmons remained a popular figure in Phoenix as a commentator for Suns television broadcasts, heeding his own advice by conveying a relentless enthusiasm.

that he would score 40 points and get 20 rebounds, and he made good on his promise by scoring 44 points and grabbing 24 boards. His team- mates were not surprised. "I knew he could," Majerle said. "He'd done it so many times. He'd carried this team so many times, and that game he came out and carried us."

Next up in the Finals were indeed the Bulls, and Barkley and Jordan took center stage. It appeared the series would be a rout after the Bulls won the first two games in Phoenix, but thanks to the three-headed attack of Barkley, Majerle, and Johnson, the Suns stayed alive by win- ning two of three games in Chicago. After claiming a 108–98 victory in Game 5, the Suns returned home with momentum. It was not to be, though. Jordan scored 33 points in Game 6 and threw a perfect pass to wide-open Bulls guard John Paxson, who hit the series-winning shot in a 99–98 Chicago win.

The Finals loss to the Bulls, though bitter, did not send the Suns into a depression. They added forward A. C. Green and center Joe Kleine and remained one of the strongest teams in the league in each of the next two seasons. However, both of those years ended with

second-round playoff defeats to the eventual NBA champion Houston Rockets. The Suns took leads in both of those series, only to see Houston bounce back and triumph in seven games.

Realizing that their losses to Houston were due largely to defensive weaknesses, the Suns made a move to exchange offense for defense, trading Majerle to Cleveland for center John "Hot Rod" Williams. The move did not pay off, as the 1995–96 Suns went 41–41 and then cleaned house, trading Barkley to the Rockets for forwards Mark Bryant, Chucky Brown, and Robert Horry.

Phoenix refused to fade, returning to the playoffs in 1997 and then posting a strong 56–26 record the following season. The 1997–98 Suns demonstrated a defensive tenacity that had long been lacking, going 45–9 when holding opponents to 100 points or fewer. However, the joy of the regular season was again overshadowed by postseason

disappointment as the Spurs and star center David
Robinson bounced the Suns in the first round.

That same pattern played out the next three seasons.
After Johnson retired in 1998 (he would return briefly
in 1999–2000), point guard Jason Kidd and, later,
Stephon Marbury, put forth some exciting offensive show-
ings, and two new coaches—former NBA guards Danny
Ainge and Scott Skiles—tried their hand at leading the
team. Neither these new players nor coaches, though,
could return the Suns to contender status.

INTRODUCING...

**KEVIN
JOHNSON**

POSITION GUARD
HEIGHT 6-FOOT-1
SUNS SEASONS
1988–98, 1999–2000

KEVIN JOHNSON WAS JUST A ROOKIE WITH POTENTIAL WHEN THE SUNS TRADED FOR HIM DURING THE 1987–88 SEASON. Phoenix personnel director Cotton Fitzsimmons believed his plodding club needed a shot in the arm, and Johnson turned out to be the perfect medicine, transforming the Suns into a high-octane, highly entertaining team. An excellent ball handler and deft passer, Johnson could shoot and pass with equal aplomb, and he asserted leadership even as one of the team's youngest players. Throughout his 12 seasons in Phoenix, Johnson averaged 17 points and 8.7 assists per game. As of 2010, he was 1 of only 3 players in NBA history to have averaged at least 20 points and 10 assists in 3 consecutive seasons. The humble Johnson credited Fitzsimmons (who became head coach in 1988) with giving him the confidence he needed to become an NBA superstar. "He told me we were going as far as I could take us," Johnson said. "That meant everything to me." After his basketball career ended, Johnson moved into politics and was elected the mayor of Sacramento, California, in 2008.

CHAPTER FIVE

RETURN OF THE RUN-AND-GUN

Strangely, it took a season of failure for the Suns to finally recognize their strengths and return to their identity as a running, high-scoring team. Phoenix went a mere 36–46 in 2001–02, but by the end of the year, new coach Frank Johnson had the team playing an up-tempo style once again. With a lineup built around Marbury, athletic forward Shawn "The Matrix" Marion, and strapping power forward Amar'e Stoudemire, the 2002–03 Suns hustled to a 44–38 mark and made the playoffs.

During the 2003–04 season, the Suns revamped their image completely. A slow start caused team management to dismiss Johnson and promote his assistant, Mike D'Antoni, to head coach. Phoenix also traded away Marbury and veteran guard Anfernee "Penny" Hardaway to create room to bring in All-Star point guard Steve Nash as a free agent prior to the 2004–05 season. The former Dallas Mavericks star (who had actually been drafted by Phoenix in 1996) was among the game's best ball handlers, and his ability to flawlessly distribute the ball while running at full speed quickly gave the Suns'

Stephon Marbury was a point guard in the mold of Kevin Johnson, known for his explosive quickness and knack for getting to the rim.

offense an air of invincibility. "It was no secret as to how good Steve was before he got here," said D'Antoni. "But once you see him operate day after day, it was a pretty awesome experience."

N ash led the league in assists in both 2004–05 and 2005–06. He also proved himself a deadly marksman, shooting higher than 50 percent from the field and 40 percent from beyond the 3-point arc. For his efforts, and for making the Suns once again a Western Conference heavyweight (with 62 and 54 wins respectively), Nash won the NBA Most Valuable Player (MVP) award in both 2005 and 2006. Nash, Marion, and Stoudemire propelled Phoenix to the doorstep of the NBA Finals both years, but the Suns came up just short, losing in the conference finals first to the Spurs, then to the Mavericks.

The Suns continued to light up NBA scoreboards in 2006–07, averaging 110 points a game, posting a 61–21 record, and winning their third straight Pacific Division title. The club seemed unbeatable at times during the season, rattling off a 15-game winning streak, then going on another tear of 17 straight. Phoenix got a big lift from guard Raja Bell, who made the NBA's All-Defensive team and connected on a career-high 205 three-pointers. Once again, though, the Suns faltered in the playoffs, losing in the second round.

THINGS COULDN'T HAVE SEEMED MUCH WORSE FOR THE SUNS THAN THEY WERE IN 2003–04, WHEN PHOENIX WENT 29–53. The team was young and rebuilding, but even the most ardent Suns supporter couldn't foresee what was about to happen in 2004–05. The Suns had just named Mike D'Antoni their new coach, and before the season, they added point guard Steve Nash and athletic swingman Quentin Richardson. Buoyed by D'Antoni's fast-paced game plan and Nash's confident on-court leadership, the Suns surged to an unbelievable 62–20 record, easily setting a franchise record with a 33-win improvement in the span of 1 year. As Nash slung the ball to such talented teammates as forwards Shawn Marion and Amar'e Stoudemire, Phoenix games became some of the hottest tickets in the NBA. The Suns streaked all the way to the Western Conference finals, and even though they were beaten in five games by the eventual NBA champion Spurs, Phoenix was a team reborn. "We feel like we bring it every night," said Nash, who was named NBA MVP, "and we demand the best of ourselves."

AMAR'E STOUDEMIRE

MANY BASKETBALL OBSERVERS THOUGHT AMAR'E STOUDEMIRE MADE A HUGE MISTAKE WHEN HE DECIDED TO ENTER THE 2002 NBA DRAFT DIRECTLY OUT OF HIS ORLANDO, FLORIDA, HIGH SCHOOL INSTEAD OF GOING TO THE UNIVERSITY OF MEMPHIS. Over the years, quite a few high-school stars had bypassed playing college basketball to go to the NBA, and most had failed. As Stoudemire quickly proved, he would not be one of them. The broad-shouldered forward was an energetic force who played fearlessly against the NBA's best big men. In his first season, Stoudemire averaged 13.5 points and 8.8 rebounds per game and was named NBA Rookie of the Year. After that, he emerged as a legitimate star by averaging 20 or more points per game in 5 of the next 6 seasons. Besides his explosive vertical leap and superb instincts, self-confidence was one of Stoudemire's greatest attributes. "Since the age of eight, I knew I would make it to the NBA," he said. "When I played ball, I was always a little bit better, a little taller, a little faster, and that kept my confidence going."

AS STEVE NASH CLAIMED TWO NBA MVP AWARDS WHILE ORCHESTRATING THE SUNS' SENSATIONAL FAST-BREAK OFFENSE, HE MADE EVERYTHING LOOK EFFORTLESS.

In reality, though, his polished performances were the result of countless hours spent in the gym perfecting his craft. When the Suns made the point guard their first choice in the 1996 NBA Draft, fans reacted with boos. "I don't look like I'm going to be a tremendous basketball player on appearance," Nash said at the time. "I probably would've booed myself too, but I'm going to be a really good player. I have a lot of faith in myself, and hopefully they'll enjoy watching me play." Nash played two unremarkable seasons for the Suns before they traded him to Dallas in 1998. Through hard work, he became one of the best point guards in the league there, and the Suns brought him back as a free agent in 2004. He immediately transformed Phoenix into a Western Conference force with his rare court vision and passing flair. In 2009, the Suns re-signed him to a two-year contract extension.

INTRODUCING...

STEVE NASH

POSITION GUARD
HEIGHT 6-FOOT-3
SUNS SEASONS
1996–98, 2004–PRESENT

M idway through the 2007–08 season, the Suns made headlines by sending Marion and another player to the Miami Heat for 14-time All-Star center Shaquille O'Neal. Although the 35-year-old giant was in the twilight of his career, Suns fans hoped that he had enough left to put Phoenix over the top. While O'Neal was a force on the boards, grabbing 10.6 rebounds a game, his acquisition was not the tonic needed. The center's slow, power-oriented style did not mesh with the Suns' fast-paced offense, and Phoenix lost in the first round of the 2008 playoffs, then missed the 2009 postseason entirely.

In the 2009 off-season, O'Neal was traded to Cleveland, and Suns fans were left hoping that Nash, Stoudemire, and guard Leandro Barbosa could turn the ship back around under new coach Alvin Gentry. "Obviously if we're a contender again, that's great—that's where everyone wants to be," Nash said. "But I think right now I'd be happy to be part of a really positive, optimistic atmosphere, be a part of a team that is really on the same page, plays together, plays hard every night, and makes the season exciting for one another and for the fans." The 2009–10 Suns fit the bill on both counts, thrilling their fans by going 54–28 and surging all the way to the conference finals before falling to the Lakers.

ince their inception in the Valley of the Sun more than 4 decades
ago, the Phoenix Suns have been a hot franchise more often than
not, making the NBA playoffs in 29 of their first 42 seasons. And
even though the grand prize of an NBA championship has thus far
eluded them, the Suns have assembled a history of stars, style, and
speed that few other franchises can match, making Arizona's capital a
hoops hotbed of the highest order.

Veteran forward Grant Hill (below) and swift guard Leandro Barbosa
(opposite) helped carry the Suns to the verge of the 2010 NBA Finals.

INDEX